HAL•LEONARD

JAZZ PLAY-ALONG®

Book and CD for B♭, E♭, C and Bass Clef Instruments

volume 87

DIXIELAND

10 TRADITIONAL SONGS

Arranged and Produced by Mark Taylor

T0079584

BOOK

CD

ISBN 978-1-4234-5472-4

HAL•LEONARD® CORPORATION

7777 W. BLUEMOUND RD. P.O. BOX 13819 MILWAUKEE, WI 53213

Visit Hal Leonard Online at
www.halleonard.com

DIXIELAND

Volume 87

Arranged and Produced by Mark Taylor

Featured Players:

Graham Breedlove–Trumpet
Tony Nalker–Piano
Jim Roberts–Bass
Leonard Cuddy–Drums

Recorded at Bias Studios, Springfield, Virginia
Bob Dawson, Engineer

HOW TO USE THE CD:

Each song has <u>two</u> tracks:

1) Split Track/Melody

Woodwind, Brass, Keyboard, and **Mallet Players** can use this track as a learning tool for melody style and inflection.

Bass Players can learn and perform with this track – remove the recorded bass track by turning down the volume on the LEFT channel.

Keyboard and **Guitar Players** can learn and perform with this track – remove the recorded piano part by turning down the volume on the RIGHT channel.

2) Full Stereo Track

Soloists or **Groups** can learn and perform with this accompaniment track with the RHYTHM SECTION only.

4

CD
❶ : SPLIT TRACK/MELODY
❷ : FULL STEREO TRACK

C VERSION

ALEXANDER'S RAGTIME BAND
FROM ALEXANDER'S RAGTIME BAND

WORDS AND MUSIC BY
IRVING BERLIN

BALLIN' THE JACK

WORDS BY JIM BURRIS
MUSIC BY CHRIS SMITH

C VERSION

THE DARKTOWN STRUTTERS' BALL

CD
◆ 7 : SPLIT TRACK/MELODY
◆ 8 : FULL STEREO TRACK

WORDS AND MUSIC BY
SHELTON BROOKS

C VERSION

BILL BAILEY, WON'T YOU PLEASE COME HOME

WORDS AND MUSIC BY
HUGHIE CANNON

C VERSION

A GOOD MAN IS HARD TO FIND

WORDS AND MUSIC BY
EDDIE GREEN

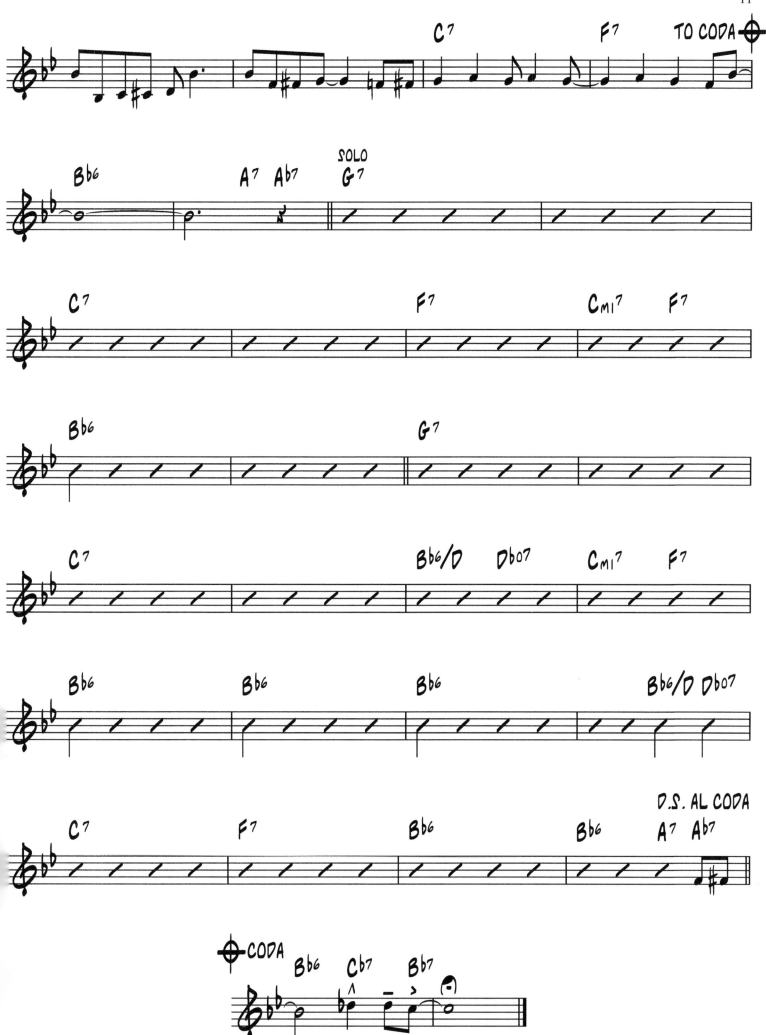

CD

 : SPLIT TRACK/MELODY

12 : FULL STEREO TRACK

ROYAL GARDEN BLUES

WORDS AND MUSIC BY CLARENCE WILLIAMS
AND SPENCER WILLIAMS

C VERSION

13

CD

THAT'S A PLENTY

WORDS BY RAY GILBERT
MUSIC BY LEW POLLACK

C VERSION

CD
15 : SPLIT TRACK/MELODY
16 : FULL STEREO TRACK

TIGER RAG
(HOLD THAT TIGER)

WORDS BY HARRY DECOSTA
MUSIC BY ORIGINAL DIXIELAND JAZZ BAND

C VERSION

TOOT, TOOT, TOOTSIE!
(GOODBYE!)

WORDS AND MUSIC BY GUS KAHN, ERNIE ERDMAN,
DAN RUSSO AND TED FIORITO

C VERSION

WHEN THE SAINTS GO MARCHING IN

WORDS BY KATHERINE E. PURVIS
MUSIC BY JAMES M. BLACK

BALLIN' THE JACK

WORDS BY JIM BURRIS
MUSIC BY CHRIS SMITH

Bb VERSION

CD
1 : SPLIT TRACK/MELODY
2 : FULL STEREO TRACK

ALEXANDER'S RAGTIME BAND

FROM ALEXANDER'S RAGTIME BAND

WORDS AND MUSIC BY
IRVING BERLIN

Bb VERSION

BILL BAILEY, WON'T YOU PLEASE COME HOME

Bb VERSION

WORDS AND MUSIC BY
HUGHIE CANNON

THE DARKTOWN STRUTTERS' BALL

WORDS AND MUSIC BY
SHELTON BROOKS

Bb VERSION

WHEN THE SAINTS GO MARCHING IN

WORDS BY KATHERINE E. PURVIS
MUSIC BY JAMES M. BLACK

Bb VERSION

A GOOD MAN IS HARD TO FIND

CD
◆ 9 : SPLIT TRACK/MELODY
◆ 10 : FULL STEREO TRACK

WORDS AND MUSIC BY
EDDIE GREEN

Bb VERSION

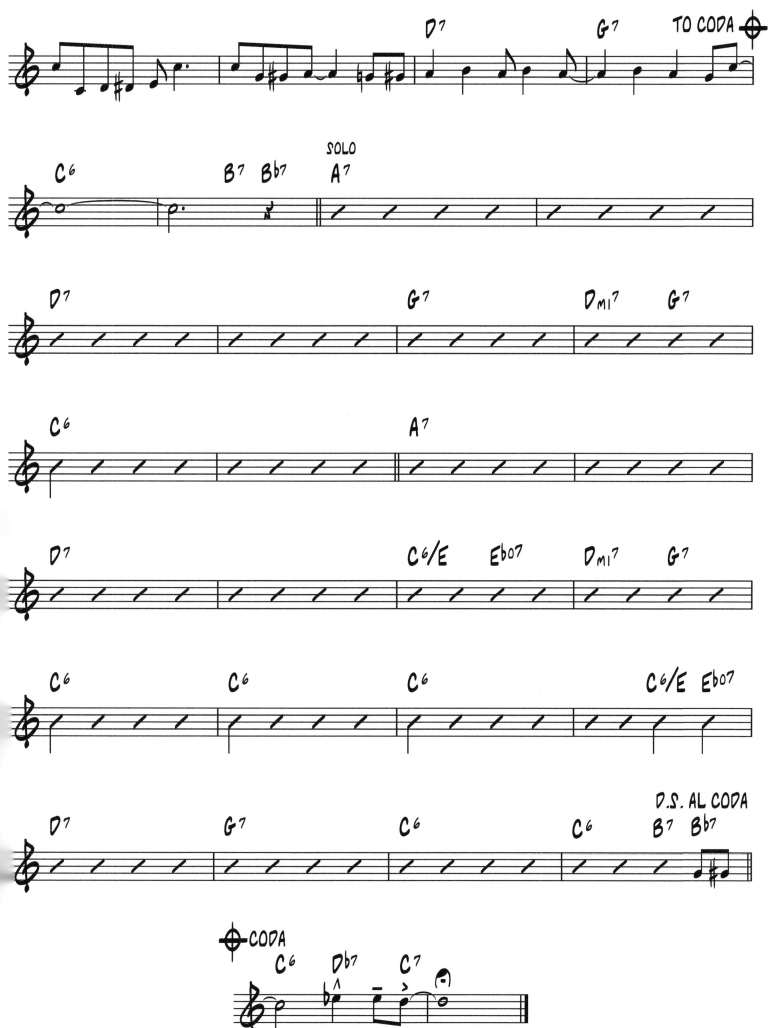

ROYAL GARDEN BLUES

WORDS AND MUSIC BY CLARENCE WILLIAMS
AND SPENCER WILLIAMS

Bb VERSION

THAT'S A PLENTY

WORDS BY RAY GILBERT
MUSIC BY LEW POLLACK

CD

⬦13: SPLIT TRACK/MELODY

⬦14: FULL STEREO TRACK

Bb VERSION

CD

15 : SPLIT TRACK/MELODY

16 : FULL STEREO TRACK

TIGER RAG
(HOLD THAT TIGER)

WORDS BY HARRY DeCOSTA
MUSIC BY ORIGINAL DIXIELAND JAZZ BAND

Bb VERSION

35

TOOT, TOOT, TOOTSIE!
(GOODBYE!)

WORDS AND MUSIC BY GUS KAHN, ERNIE ERDMAN,
DAN RUSSO AND TED FIORITO

CD

17 : SPLIT TRACK/MELODY
18 : FULL STEREO TRACK

Bb VERSION

CD
1: SPLIT TRACK/MELODY
2: FULL STEREO TRACK

ALEXANDER'S RAGTIME BAND

FROM ALEXANDER'S RAGTIME BAND

WORDS AND MUSIC BY
IRVING BERLIN

Eb VERSION

BALLIN' THE JACK

WORDS BY JIM BURRIS
MUSIC BY CHRIS SMITH

THE DARKTOWN STRUTTERS' BALL

CD
7 : SPLIT TRACK/MELODY
8 : FULL STEREO TRACK

WORDS AND MUSIC BY
SHELTON BROOKS

Eb VERSION

42

BILL BAILEY, WON'T YOU PLEASE COME HOME

Eb VERSION

WORDS AND MUSIC BY
HUGHIE CANNON

TO CODA

A GOOD MAN IS HARD TO FIND

WORDS AND MUSIC BY
EDDIE GREEN

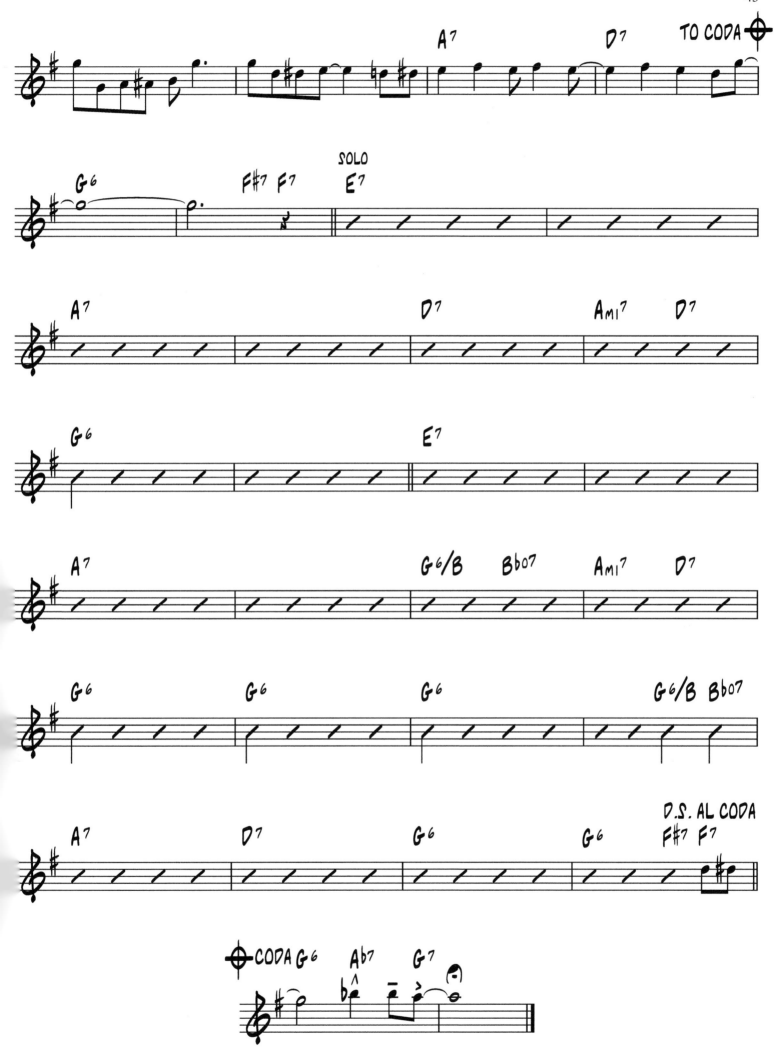

ROYAL GARDEN BLUES

CD
- **11** : SPLIT TRACK/MELODY
- **12** : FULL STEREO TRACK

Eb VERSION

WORDS AND MUSIC BY CLARENCE WILLIAMS
AND SPENCER WILLIAMS

THAT'S A PLENTY

CD

13 : SPLIT TRACK/MELODY

14 : FULL STEREO TRACK

WORDS BY RAY GILBERT
MUSIC BY LEW POLLACK

Eb VERSION

TIGER RAG
(HOLD THAT TIGER)

WORDS BY HARRY DeCOSTA
MUSIC BY ORIGINAL DIXIELAND JAZZ BAND

TOOT, TOOT, TOOTSIE!
(GOODBYE!)

WORDS AND MUSIC BY GUS KAHN, ERNIE ERDMAN,
DAN RUSSO AND TED FIORITO

Eb VERSION

53

WHEN THE SAINTS GO MARCHING IN

CD
19 : SPLIT TRACK/MELODY
20 : FULL STEREO TRACK

WORDS BY KATHERINE E. PURVIS
MUSIC BY JAMES M. BLACK

Eb VERSION

BALLIN' THE JACK

WORDS BY JIM BURRIS
MUSIC BY CHRIS SMITH

ALEXANDER'S RAGTIME BAND

FROM ALEXANDER'S RAGTIME BAND

WORDS AND MUSIC BY
IRVING BERLIN

CD

⑤ : SPLIT TRACK/MELODY
⑥ : FULL STEREO TRACK

BILL BAILEY, WON'T YOU PLEASE COME HOME

𝄢: C VERSION

WORDS AND MUSIC BY
HUGHIE CANNON

THE DARKTOWN STRUTTERS' BALL

WHEN THE SAINTS GO MARCHING IN

CD
19 : SPLIT TRACK/MELODY
20 : FULL STEREO TRACK

WORDS BY KATHERINE E. PURVIS
MUSIC BY JAMES M. BLACK

9: C VERSION

A GOOD MAN IS HARD TO FIND

WORDS AND MUSIC BY
EDDIE GREEN

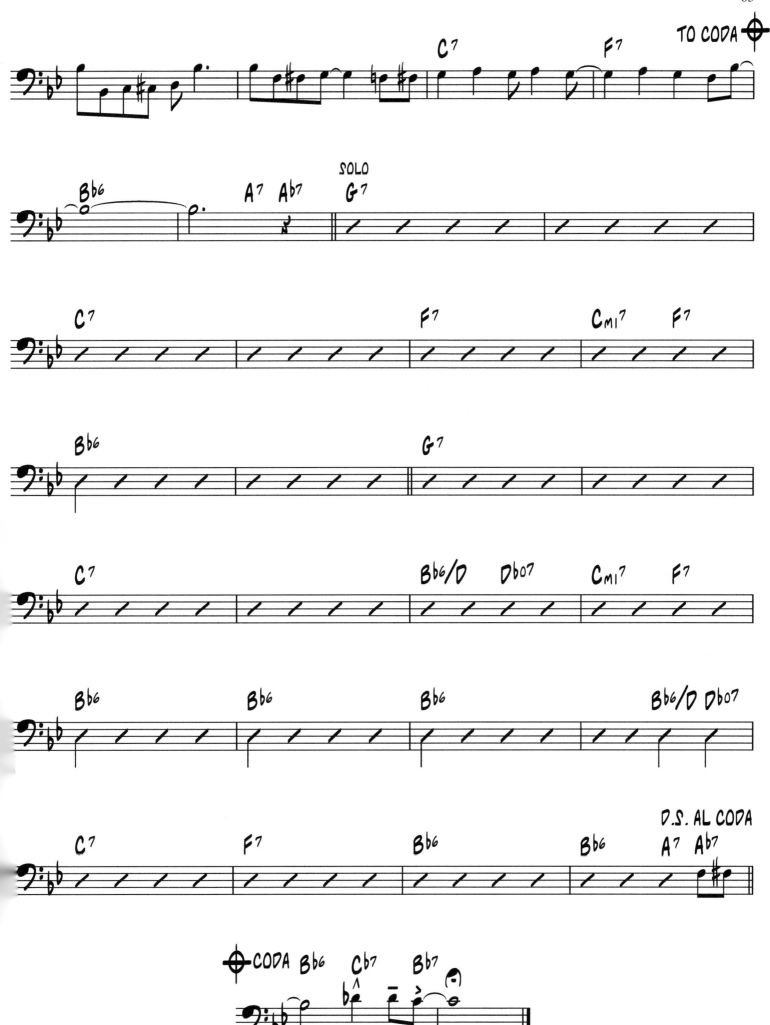

ROYAL GARDEN BLUES

CD
11 : SPLIT TRACK/MELODY
12 : FULL STEREO TRACK

WORDS AND MUSIC BY CLARENCE WILLIAMS
AND SPENCER WILLIAMS

C VERSION

THAT'S A PLENTY

CD
◆13 : SPLIT TRACK/MELODY
◆14 : FULL STEREO TRACK

𝄢: C VERSION

WORDS BY RAY GILBERT
MUSIC BY LEW POLLACK

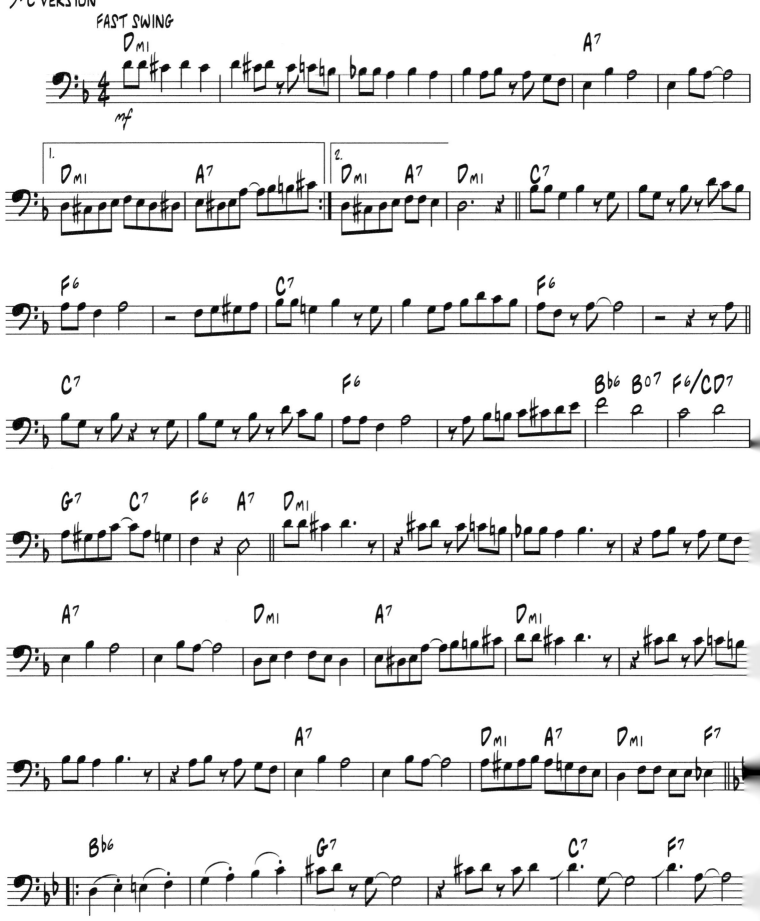

CD

◆15 : SPLIT TRACK/MELODY

◆16 : FULL STEREO TRACK

TIGER RAG
(HOLD THAT TIGER)

WORDS BY HARRY DeCOSTA
MUSIC BY ORIGINAL DIXIELAND JAZZ BAND

𝄢: C VERSION

CD
17 : SPLIT TRACK/MELODY
18 : FULL STEREO TRACK

𝄢 : C VERSION

TOOT, TOOT, TOOTSIE!
(GOODBYE!)

WORDS AND MUSIC BY GUS KAHN, ERNIE ERDMAN,
DAN RUSSO AND TED FIORITO

ERIC BAUMGARTNER'S JAZZ IT·UP! SERIES

Eric Baumgartner's *Jazz It Up! Series* are jazz arrangements of well-known tunes that both experienced and beginning jazz pianists will enjoy. The stylized pieces are intentionally written without chord symbols or improvisation sections, although pianists are encouraged to experiment and explore!

Christmas
TWELVE CAROLS
Mid-Intermediate Level
Deck the Hall • God Rest Ye Merry, Gentlemen • O Christmas Tree • The Coventry Carol • Good King Wenceslas • Jingle Bells, and more!

00349037 Book/Audio . $12.99

Familiar Favorites
SEVEN FOLK SONGS
Mid-Intermediate Level
All Through the Night • The Erie Canal • Greensleeves • La Cucaracha • Londonderry Air • Scarborough Fair • When the Saints Go Marching In.

00416778 Book/Audio ... $9.95

Classics
SIX CLASSICAL FAVES
Mid-Intermediate Level
Funeral March of a Marionette (Gounod) • Habanera (Bizet) • Nutcracker Rock (Tchaikovsky) • Song for the New World (Dvořák) • Spinning Song (Ellmenreich) • Symphonic Swing (Mozart).

00416867 Book/Audio ... $9.99

Standards
SEVEN FAVORITE CLASSICS
Mid-Intermediate Level
Ain't Misbehavin' • Autumn Leaves • Don't Get Around Much Anymore • God Bless' the Child • One Note Samba • Stormy Weather • Take Five.

00416903 Book/Audio . $14.99

View sample pages and hear audio excerpts online at www.halleonard.com

EXCLUSIVELY DISTRIBUTED BY

HAL•LEONARD®

Prices, contents, and availability subject to change without notice.